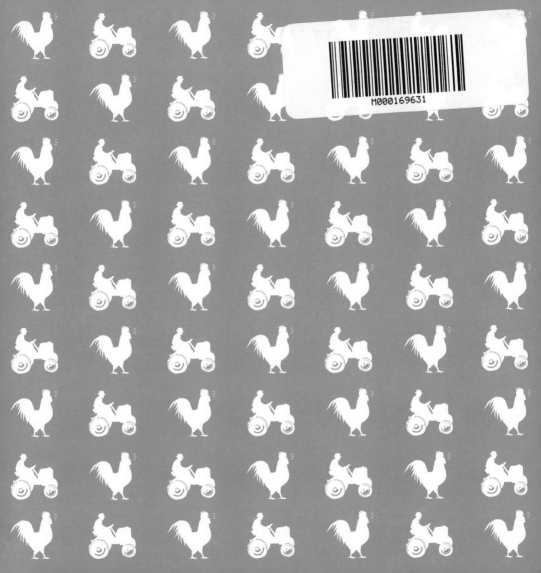

ADVICE

from a

COUNTRY
FARMER

ADVICE

from a

COUNTRY
FARMER

ROY ENGLISH

GIBBS SMITH
TO ENRICH AND INSPIRE HUMANKIND

First Edition
15 14 13 12 11   5 4 3 2 1

Text © 2011 Roy English

Published by
Gibbs Smith
P.O. Box 667
Layton, Utah 84041

1.800.835.4993 orders
www.gibbs-smith.com

Designed by Black Eye Design
Printed and bound in Hong Kong
Gibbs Smith books are printed on paper produced from
sustainable PEFC-certified forest/controlled wood source.
Learn more at www.pefc.org.

Library of Congress Cataloging-in-Publication Data

English, Roy, 1943-
  Advice from a country farmer / Roy English. — 1st ed.
    p. cm.
  ISBN 978-1-4236-1860-7
 1. American wit and humor. 2. Country life—Humor. I. Title.
  PN6165.E54 2011
  818'.5402—dc22
                          2011004373

DON'T ARGUE

just for the hell of it.

To a farmer,
RETIRE
is something you
do to a tractor.

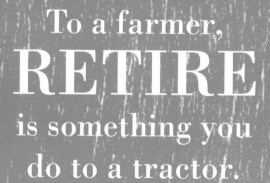

HORSEPOWER
IS NO SUBSTITUTE
FOR HORSE SENSE.

7

Most farmers work only half a day; the other twelve hours they do *other* stuff.

Farmers

BELIEVE IN MIRACLES.

They see them every day.

LIFE IS SIMPLER :
WHEN YOU PLOW
AROUND THE STUMPS.

Mamas,
don't let your cowboys grow up to be babies.

11

You can shear a sheep every year.
You can butcher him only once.

The *only* farmers
who sleep late are
in the cemetery.

A fella who BRAGS
about his
OWN HUMILITY
will LIE about
ANYTHING.

MEANNESS

DON'T

HAPPEN

OVERNIGHT.

Don't judge
a farmer by the

SIZE

of his tractor.

16

FORGIVE
YOUR ENEMIES.
It messes with their heads.

Old farmers
never die.
Their lug nuts
just get rusty.

It don't take a very big man
to carry a grudge.

YOU CAN'T UNSAY A
CRUEL THING.

Nobody works harder
than a farmer, except maybe a
FARMER'S WIFE.

Every path
has some puddles.

A rooster that
crows at midnight
*won't make it
past Sunday.*

FARMERS KNOW STUFF THAT AIN'T WROTE DOWN NOWHERE.

When you wallow with pigs,
EXPECT TO GET DIRTY.

The best sermons
ARE LIVED,
not preached.

A lazy fella
is about as
helpful as the
"o" in opossum.

27

Most of the stuff folks worry about
NEVER HAPPENS.

FARMING IS GOD'S WORK,
sure as preaching.

A FARM DOG KNOWS
when to bark
when to bite,
and when to stay
under the porch.

It's better to dig
a pond in a valley
than on a hilltop.

A ROOSTER IS A MAGICIAN.
He can turn an egg into a chicken.

A tractor is just a
mule with tires,
but it costs more to feed.

Anyone who wants to live
happily ever after
had best tend to it daily.

34

Don't work for an outfit
YOU DON'T BELIEVE IN.

Get rid of your
showhorses
and keep your
workhorses.

36

MAKE HAY
while the sun shines.

DEBT IS A SHOVEL.

It can dig a well or a grave.

It's best to roll down
the truck window
BEFORE YOU SPIT.

A MULE CAN'T HELP IT IF HIS HELP IT IF HIS DADDY IS A JACKASS.

Visit your kin,

but don't move in with them.

41

The two
MOST DANGEROUS FUMES
are gasoline fumes
and perfumes.

HOOT OWLS AND BANKERS SLEEP WITH ONE EYE OPEN.

To forgive an *enemy* is easy.
To forgive a *friend* is hard.

You can't blame a
worm for not wanting
to go fishing.

A fella who can
HOLD HIS TONGUE
HAS A GOOD GRIP
on the situation.

NOTHING IS QUITE AS SILLY AS AN EDUCATED FOOL.

The only way to
learn with your
mouth open is to
read aloud.

FARMERS and BALL PLAYERS
are only as good as last season's
PERFORMANCE.

THE LAZY
CALL THE
SKILLFUL LUCKY.

50

DON'T STOP TRYING.

If you fall down seven times
and get up six,
you might as well have
stayed down the first time.

Country fences need to be
horse-high, *pig-tight*,
and *bull-strong*.

No riverboat gambler
ever wagered as heavily
AS THE FAMILY FARMER.

MOST SHORTCUTS
ARE DEAD ENDS.

54

In farming and politics, **timing is everything.**

DON'T TELL A ROOSTER HE'S NOT RESPONSIBLE FOR THE SUN COMING UP.

Make yourself useful.

If you can't weave a blanket, mend a sock.

When you
surprise
an animal,
it might
surprise
you back.

CROOKED POSTS MAKE CROOKED FENCES.

A FARMER IS

part carpenter,
mechanic,
scientist,
banker,
weatherman,
veterinarian,
preacher, and
gambler.

60

DON'T sell your tractor to buy a plow.

WHEN YOU HAVE TO
MAKE A BIG DECISION,
SLEEP ON IT.

62

WANTS and NEEDS

are two different things.

The first fella to suggest
pitching horseshoes
must have gotten
some funny looks.

A cow kick is a
HAYMAKER.

A mule kick is a
WIDOWMAKER.

It's hard to fool
AN OLD FARMER.

BETTER LOCKS MAKE BETTER THIEVES.

FARMERS DO IT

IN THE FIELD.

When all else fails,
blame the devil.

TO HAVE a good neighbor,
BE a good neighbor.

70

Strapping a saddle
onto a pig
don't make him
a cow pony.

BELIEVING
in something makes it possible,
not easy.

Around animals, a calm demeanor IS BEST.

DON'T

name a pig
you plan to eat.

To a farmer,

a fertile field is hallowed ground.

CUT YOUR LOSSES.

Know when to
debit cash and
credit experience.

Being sorry and
being sorry you got caught
are two different things.

WHEN FRYING
FROG LEGS,
PUT A LID
ON THE SKILLET.

HOW TO MAKE A SMALL FORTUNE
IN THE HORSE BUSINESS:
start with a large fortune.

Having a 10 percent
chance of rain for
ten days don't mean
there's a 100 percent
chance of rain.

KEEP SKUNKS AND BANKERS AT A DISTANCE.

PLOWING A FIELD

gives a body time to think, or not.

To a farmer,
wind blowing through
cornstalks sounds a
lot like applause.

DRIFTERS ARE DRIFTERS FOR A REASON.

DON'T PLANT
more than you can
harvest.

DON'T HARVEST
more than you can sell,
use, or give away.

It takes more than
wearing a John Deere cap
and chewing on a straw
to be a farmer.

A BONEHEAD BLUNDER IS NOT A TOTAL LOSS IF YOU LEARN SOMETHING FROM IT.

A FARMER
goes to sleep with the
chickens so he can
WAKE UP WITH
THE ROOSTER.

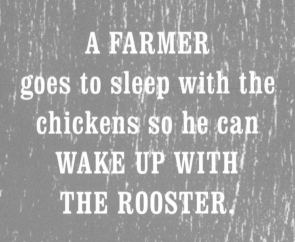

God made us with

TWO EARS

and only

ONE TONGUE.

That should tell
us something.

A thirty-minute nap after lunch
will aid a man's digestion,
improve his attitude,
and increase productivity.
A sixty-minute nap will
ruin him for the day.

SOMEONE WHO
CLAIMS TO WALK ON
WATER IS EITHER A
HYPOCRITE OR AN
ESKIMO.

Farmers understand
THE CIRCLE OF LIFE
better than most.

If Jerusalem got *a little more rain*,
Jesus would likely have been a farmer.

THE DIFFERENCE BETWEEN FAST WORK AND HURRIED WORK IS KNOW~HOW.

94

DON'T CORNER something that's **MEANER THAN YOU.**

YOU CAN'T BLAME THE ROOSTER for not wanting to invite the preacher for Sunday dinner.

People forget
WHAT GOOD FARMERS
our founding fathers were.

When you
lose your temper,
you find stuff
you didn't know
you had.

Age does not

GUARANTEE

WISDOM

any more than youth

GUARANTEES

AMBITION.

IF FARMERS STOPPED
GROWING TOBACCO,
PEOPLE WOULD JUST
SMOKE LETTUCE.

PICKLES and PEOPLE
are SWEET or SOUR
depending on whether they
spent their early days soaked
in SUGAR or VINEGAR.

A horse that can't be broke
WINDS UP AS A BAR OF SOAP.

IF A GOOSE LAID A GOLDEN EGG, YOU'D LIKELY NEVER FIND IT FOR THE POOP.

Where I come from, they **hang whiners.**

It takes
TWO THINGS
to do a job:
to start and to finish.

YOU CAN PUT
LIPSTICK ON A PIG,
BUT NOT ON A
CHICKEN.

There's no use in knowing
how to do something
UNLESS YOU
DO IT.

ENTHUSIASM

without know-how is a bumpy ride.

LUST
SOMETIMES
LEADS TO LOVE,
SOMETIMES NOT.

Except for mules,
most of God's creatures
want to leave something
to their kids.

WE FORGET THE STUFF
we need to remember
and remember the stuff
WE NEED TO FORGET.

WHEN YOU GET SICK,
if you go to the doctor
you'll probably get well
within seven days.
If you don't go, it will
likely take a week.

DON'T LOAN MONEY TO A FRIEND. GIVE IT TO HIM. YOU'LL HAVE A BETTER CHANCE OF BEING REPAID.

THE ONLY CLOCK

that matters to a farmer is a sundial.

Many a
stickery problem
has been solved
on a tractor.

WHATEVER THE MALADY OF OLD AGE, ENTHUSIASM IS THE BEST TONIC.

LEARN YOUR SOIL TO KNOW YOUR CROP:

black for cotton,
red for peanuts,
brown for cantaloupes,
gray for tomatoes.

YOU CAN'T plant cotton and expect to get cotton candy.

DON'T SMOKE
IN THE HAYLOFT.

THE FIRST FELLA
who pickled pig's feet
must have been
MIGHTY HUNGRY.

FARMERS FEED THE WORLD.

A GIRL

has to like a guy a lot to go
to the prom on a tractor.

MOST YOUNG PEOPLE LEAVE THE FARM FOR OTHER FIELDS.

The cost of a wedding has little to do with the quality of a

MARRIAGE.

DON'T TAKE TOO MUCH PRIDE IN BEING A GOOD LOSER.

DON'T
SKINNY DIP

with snapping turtles.

THE MANY FACES OF ROY ENGLISH:

Farmer/Rancher

Attorney

State lawmaker

Judge

Singer/Songwriter

Novelist/Screenwriter

The author invites reader response at
JudgeRoyEnglish@aol.com.